W9-CKI-295

Girls'

VOLLEYBALL

by Jon Ackerman

GIRLS'
SportsZone

Published by ABDO Publishing Company, PO Box 398166, Minneapolis, MN 55439. Copyright © 2014 by Abdo Consulting Group, Inc. International copyrights reserved in all countries. No part of this book may be reproduced in any form without written permission from the publisher. SportsZone™ is a trademark and logo of ABDO Publishing Company.

Printed in the United States of America,
North Mankato, Minnesota

052013
092013

Editor: Chrös McDougall
Series Designer: Marie Tupy

Photo Credits: Steve Cukrov/Shutterstock Images, cover, 1; Margaret Bowles/AP Images, 5, 13, 29, 37; Andy Wong/AP Images, 6; Sipa via AP Images, 8; Jeff Roberson/AP Images, 10, 14, 17, 21, 30, 32, 41; Dave Martin/AP Images, 19, 39, 42; Elsa/Getty Images, 22; The World-Herald, Matt Miller/AP Images, 24; Robert DeBerry/AP Images, 27; Luca Bruno/AP Images, 34; Shutterstock Images/Red Line Editorial, Inc., 44

Library of Congress Control Number: 2013932499

Cataloging-in-Publication Data

Ackerman, Jon.
 Girls' volleyball / Jon Ackerman.
   p. cm. -- (Girls' sportszone)
 ISBN 978-1-61783-991-7 (lib. bdg.)
 Includes bibliographical references and index.
 1. Volleyball for girls--Juvenile literature. I. Title.
 796.325--dc23

                                                                    2013932499

Table of Contents

chapter 1

Serving with Logan Tom

L ogan Tom played in her fourth Olympic Games for Team USA in
2012. Yet one of the most impressive serving performances in her
career took place five months earlier. Tom was suited up for her
professional team in Turkey that February night. Her squad led 15–9 in the
first set when she stepped back to serve.

Tom began approximately 20 feet (6.01 m) behind the end line.
Bending forward, she bounced the ball three quick times. Then she spun it
in her left hand. At the referee's whistle, she began her serve.

Tom tossed the ball high into the air with her right hand and began
moving toward the far left corner of the court. As she approached the end
line, Tom leapt into the air. She swung her right arm overhead. At the peak

Logan Tom goes up to serve for Team USA at the 2012 Olympic Games in London.

of her jump, Tom's right palm hit the top half of the ball. Hitting the ball like that created topspin, causing the ball to dip while in flight.

And the ball dipped so sharply that it clipped the top of the net before rolling over to the other side. The opposing team managed to save the play and set up a back-row attack. But the return shot flew into the net. Tom's challenging serve had forced a difficult play. And she was not done yet.

Tom continued to do the same routine before each serve. And she continued to serve the ball to nearly the same spot each time. That spot was a little deeper than the middle of the opponent's side of the court. It proved to be a good spot to aim for.

Logan Tom is a fierce competitor whether playing for Team USA or a professional club team.

Tom's second serve was received near the floor. But the setter could not get to the ball to continue the play. Tom's third serve landed untouched right in her key location. Her fourth serve hit a player in the leg as the player tried to reach for it. Her fifth serve traveled down the line. The opposing player could only get a hand on it as she dove. Then Tom's sixth serve became her fourth straight ace. The player in the center of the court got only an arm on the ball.

Tom's teammates began to get excited. But Tom never smiled throughout this run. That was because she was not done. The opposing libero received Tom's seventh serve. But the libero's pass did not allow for a strong attack. The team played the ball over the net, but Tom's squad quickly scored another point.

The opponents were unable to create a clean pass on Tom's eighth serve. Then her ninth

SERVING STYLES

There are two main types of serves in volleyball. The easiest serve is a standing serve, or float serve. This is when a player holds the ball in her off hand. Then she swings her dominant hand like a pendulum and hits the ball with the palm of her hand. A topspin serve is more advanced. This is when the player tosses the ball into the air. She then hits the ball's top side with her palm while flicking her wrist forward. The force of this forward rotation causes the ball to dip more quickly. These topspin serves can also be executed while jumping. The most advanced players also take a running start to their jump.

serve landed untouched in the middle of the court. The opponents looked at each other in disbelief. The opposing libero raised her arms, wondering what to do.

Now it was match point. And on Tom's tenth serve, the other team formed its strongest attack yet. But Tom's team made a nice dig to save the play. Fittingly, Tom won the set with a powerful spike from behind the attack line. Final score: 25–9.

That was just one game in a career that has lasted more than 10 years. Yet it is proof for why Tom is one of the elite servers in the world.

Sheilla Castro of Brazil prepares to serve from well behind the end line at the 2008 Olympic Games in Beijing, China.

It All Starts with Serving

Serving is the way every rally is started. It is also the best way to control a match. If a team can serve tough—meaning hard and accurate—it can put the opponent at a serious disadvantage. Sometimes that results in an ace. Or if an opponent struggles to control a serve, its first pass will be off the mark. That makes a set and ensuing spike more difficult to execute.

At the highest levels, coaches often form strategy around their best servers. Sometimes great servers are brought into the rotation just to serve. Coaches generally have an idea of the other team's strengths and weaknesses. So teams aim to send serves toward the players who have a difficult time passing. This requires a great deal of skill by the server. Accurate serves are the mark of a good squad.

There are other strategies for serve location. A team might notice that the opposing setter struggles to get to the back of the court. In that case, the serving team might repeatedly serve the ball to that area. Or a server might try to catch the other team off guard by placing a ball just barely over the net. Deep and short serving is especially common in beach volleyball, where only two players are on a team. Another strategy is to serve the ball as hard as possible. Even the best players can struggle to control a hard-driven ball if it arrives more quickly than they expected.

Italy's Jenny Barazza begins her serve during the 2012 Olympic Games in London.

Quick Tip: Serve It Solo

Serving is one of the few volleyball skills that can be practiced alone. One way to practice serving is by setting up a target, such as a cone or a chair, on one side of the net. Then gather as many balls as possible on the other side. Use those balls to practice serving toward the target. After hitting it 10 times, move the target to another area and repeat. Serving might look like one of the simplest skills, but good serving requires accuracy. That comes from practice.

Once the mechanics of serving are mastered, serving accurately is another test. Hard serves are especially challenging to keep in bounds. Weber State women's volleyball coach Tom Peterson has some simple advice for those working on serving accurately. "Navigating the fine line between tough serves and missed serves is made easier by devoting due time and attention to working on the serve, both in and out of practice," he said. That is the approach that helped Tom become one of the best servers in the world.

2

Digging with Nicole Davis

T eam USA opened its quarterfinal match against the Dominican Republic at the 2012 Olympic Games by winning the first set. Then the Dominican Republic took a 10–9 lead in the second set.

The Dominicans nearly took a two-point lead. A spike sped past the Americans' two-person block and headed for the back corner. But at the last instant, Team USA libero Nicole Davis lunged to her right and stuck out her right arm. Falling to her knee, she made just enough contact with the ball to pass it nicely toward the net. One of her teammates quickly tipped it over, and the Americans eventually won the rally. That evened the score.

Team USA coach Hugh McCutcheon looks on as Nicole Davis digs in the gold-medal match at the 2012 Olympic Games.

Another great rally occurred on the next play. The Dominican Republic again tried to attack the back corner. Davis responded once more. She brought her arms together and squatted so low that her left knee touched the floor. Then her forearms snuck under the ball right before it would have hit the ground. Davis's pass floated perfectly to the middle of her side of the court. The setter was easily able to get under it. She set a pass for a backline attacker, who crushed a spike. Team USA eventually won that rally as well.

That gave the Americans the lead. And they never looked back. Team USA held on to win the second set. Then it won the match by

As the libero, Nicole Davis (6) wore a different uniform than her US teammates at the 2012 Olympic Games.

winning the third set as well. The United States' march to the Olympic silver medal continued.

Those key plays were the result of Davis's skill and experience. The 2012 Olympic Games were her second with Team USA. Before that she won two consecutive college national championships with her University of Southern California Trojans. They even went 35–0 during her senior year in 2003. So she had plenty of experience in making key plays.

Against the Dominican Republic, Davis showcased great positioning. She was in the right position to defend against a spike to those corners. She also had very quick reactions. That is very important against opponents with strong attackers. Perhaps most important, however, was Davis's technique. Over years of practice she knew how to

LIFE OF A LIBERO

Nicole Davis is easy to spot. She was the shortest player (5 feet, 4 inches) on the 2008 and 2012 US Olympic volleyball teams. She also wore a different-colored jersey from her teammates. That is because she was the team's libero, also known as a "ball control specialist." The libero plays only in the back row. She cannot hit the ball while it is higher than the net and cannot handset in front of the attack line. But liberos still get plenty of action. Davis was the second-ranked libero at the 2012 Olympic Games with 97 digs and 224 "excellent" receptions in 27 sets. Excellent receptions are balls that are sent right to the setter.

delicately hit the ball so that it would stay in play. A bad dig could send the ball out of play or force her teammate to make a difficult set. But with a careful dig and an accurate spike, her team could set up a powerful attack. The Dominican Republic found that out the hard way when playing Davis and Team USA in 2012.

Receiving and Digging

There are three primary types of passes: the serve receive, the set, and the dig. The serve receive and the dig are most similar. Both are important because they keep the play alive. The serve receive and dig also lead to a set. And a good set leads to a better attack. That is how teams win matches.

The serving team has the first opportunity to set the tone for a rally. The serve receive is the opposing team's first opportunity to change the tone and take control. A good serve receive passes the ball to the setter. The setter then sets the ball for another player to attack. The first goal for a serve receive is to keep the ball in play. After that, the second goal should be to get the ball to a teammate as accurately as possible.

Mike Hebert was the women's volleyball coach at the University of Minnesota from 1996 to 2010. "A quick offensive tempo begins as a concept on the coach's clipboard," he said. "It can become reality only if the team can pass accurately."

Once a rally is in motion, digging is often the best bet to keep it in motion. Digging is when a player stops an opposing spike or attack from touching the ground. It is similar to a serve receive. One difference is that a spike usually comes from the opposing frontcourt. That means the ball

Nicole Davis gets low and puts her entire body into a dig against Turkey during the 2012 Olympic Games.

can come in at sharper angles and at faster speeds. At the highest levels, defensive players have only a split-second to react to a hard-driven spike.

Digs and serve receives are usually executed with two arms out in front of the body. The goal is to make contact with the ball with the inside of the forearms. However, a player might not have time to get in position. Sometimes players need to dive to reach a quickly falling ball. Or players might only have time to stick out an arm to try to make contact. As long as she keeps the ball off the ground and gets it to a teammate, the rally continues.

A good passer needs to have visual, physical, and mental skills. The player's eyes need to see the ball well. She has to watch from the moment it leaves the opponent's hand until it arrives on her own forearms. A players' footwork helps her get in position to receive the serve. Her arms must absorb the contact while sending the ball back into the air.

RECEIVING STRATEGY

As teams become more advanced, coaches may decide that only a few players receive serves. The most common strategy is a five-player system. This is where everyone except the setter is responsible for a certain area of the court. In a four-player strategy, two players cover the right side (one in front, one in back) and two players cover the left side (one front, one back). And if a coach decides to have only three people receive serves, one would be in charge of the left side, one in the center, and one on the right.

Quick Tip: Flat Forearms

To get a feel for how the arms should be held when passing, hold a board that is 8 inches wide (20.3 cm) by 10 inches (25.4 cm) long. Each hand grabs a top corner, with the sides of the board against the forearms. Lock the elbows. This is how stiff the arms should be. In an actual match, bring the hands together, but visualize the arms being as stiff as that board.

A good passer also must have confidence. This comes from hours of proper practice. She also must have the ability to forget any mistakes from the past. In volleyball, it is common for a team to serve at a player who just made an error. That person might continue to make mistakes if she cannot get the bad play out of her mind.

Juliana Silva of Brazil stretches out to dig during beach volleyball action at the 2012 Olympic Games.

chapter 3

Setting with Lindsey Berg

Lindsey Berg rarely receives a serve. That is because the three-time US Olympian is a setter. So she follows her team's rotation. But when the ball is served she quickly races from her spot in the rotation to the center of the court, just a few feet from the net. Then she immediately turns her body toward the ball. That is because she knows the first pass is coming her way. The setter then decides who gets to attack. Her decision has to be made in an instant.

Berg makes a decision while she positions herself under the ball. As it falls, she often lifts her left leg and jumps slightly off her right foot. In the air, she positions her body so it is square with where she wants to pass. Then the ball is in her fingertips for a split second before it is sent back up.

Team USA setter Lindsey Berg sets the ball for a teammate to hit during the 2012 Olympic gold-medal match against Brazil.

21

Berg straightens both arms as she completes the set. If she wants the ball to go forward, she rounds her back and follows through in that direction. When she wants it to go backward, she arches her back and follows through. If the pass only needs to travel a few feet, Berg simply flicks her wrists in that direction. When her intended attacker is on the front line, Berg aims her pass to fall a couple feet off the net. For a back-row hitter, her pass falls a few feet in front of the attack line.

Lindsey Berg of the United States sets the ball to a teammate during the 2012 Olympic Games.

One of Berg's finest nights came at the 2011 World Cup. The US women's team was ranked second in the world. And on the tournament's first day the United States beat top-ranked Brazil. With 53 assists on the night, Berg was the star of the match. She directly set up more than half of the team's 94 points in the match. Five US players scored 10 or more points. That meant Berg distributed her passes very evenly.

Berg's strong performance that 2011 day helped Team USA defeat Brazil on a big stage. Then the US team went on to finish second in the tournament. Brazil ended up fifth. Those results were enough to give the United States the world's top ranking. It marked the first time in four years that the Brazilian women were not number one. Berg has enjoyed a long career with matches like that. The Hawaii native starred at the University of Minnesota from 1998 to 2001. Then she began a

NEAR-PERFECT ACCURACY

Lindsey Berg finished the 2012 Olympic Games ranked fourth in the Best Setter category. That ranking is based on the number of running sets the players execute per set. A running set is when the attacker hits against one or fewer blockers. But each of the three setters ahead of Berg recorded more faults. In 575 total setting attempts, Berg faulted just once. The only setter to be more accurate was South Korea's Kim Sa-Nee. She had no faults in 619 setting attempts.

professional and international career that included three Olympic Games, from 2004 to 2012.

Setting and the Setter

By definition, a set is a pass in which the ball is positioned for a teammate to attack. That makes it very important in any volleyball match. A well-placed set helps the attacker make a good shot. Setting also involves a lot of strategy. So the setter constantly has to be aware of surroundings. Which teammates might be ready to attack? Where are they? Where are the opposing players lined up? When a team scores a point on a powerful spike, there was usually a good set just before.

Setter Lauren Cook sets the ball to a University of Nebraska teammate during a 2012 game against the University of Washington.

There are a few different ways to set up a teammate. The most basic method is the forearm pass. This is also called a bump set. It is often used at the youth levels. Bump sets are also common when a team's first pass is too low for the setter to do an overhead set. Forearm passes are also common in beach volleyball. The two beach players have a lot of ground to cover. So they are not always able to get under a ball for an overhead set.

The overhead set is the most common type of pass at the high school level and higher. This is when the player softly lifts the ball up using her fingertips. A player can be more accurate using her fingertips rather than her forearms. Ideally, any set will leave the ball a few feet off the net. That allows the attacking teammate to follow through on an overhand swing without touching the net.

There is a lot of strategy behind setting. Most importantly the setter wants to get the ball to

THE QUARTERBACK OF THE COURT

Every team needs a leader. In football, it is typically the quarterback. In indoor volleyball, it is generally the setter. Like a quarterback, the setter touches the ball on nearly every play. When a ball is received, the setter usually makes the next touch if she can get to the ball. From there, she decides who attacks. Then she does the best she can to set up the attackers. The setter knows from where her hitters like to attack. Coaches often help the setter strategize.

FAULTS

One of the most common faults called on setters is the two-handed touch. This occurs when one hand contacts the ball before the other. The hands must remain evenly spaced until the ball leaves the fingers. Another common fault for setters is a lift. This is when the player holds the ball too long. If a player tries to hand set the ball from either too low or too high, she is more likely to lift or carry the ball.

one of her team's best attackers. Those players are often based on the far sides of the court. The setter also has to keep the defensive players in mind, too. If a set is too obvious, opposing players can get in better position to block.

One way to keep opponents guessing is by using a quick set. This short pass goes to the player closest to the setter. It requires precise timing because the attacker does not have much time to judge the flight of the ball. Another tricky play is the back set. This is when a setter passes the ball behind her without looking at a specific player.

The best volleyball teams do many things to try to disguise attacks. Often multiple players will begin attack approaches even before the set. That gives the setter several options to pick from. It also means the opposing blockers cannot key in on one potential attacker.

The setter is one of the most important players on a volleyball team. She has to be both accurate and alert. In a split second the setter must

Quick Tip: Strengthen the Fingers

To develop stronger fingers and improve setting, try doing wall push-ups on your fingertips. Stand about three feet (.91 m) away from a wall. Then extend your arms until the fingertips touch the wall. Let your weight fall forward, then push yourself up from there. As you become stronger, hold a ball against the wall and push up off the ball. Stronger fingers will help you better place the ball while setting.

decide where to place the ball and then physically send it there. It takes a lot of hard work and practice to reach Berg's level. But having a good setter can be the difference between a good team and a great team.

This high school volleyball player prepares to set the ball to a teammate who is about to leap into the air for a spike.

chapter 4

Spiking with Destinee Hooker

S outh Korea just would not quit. The South Koreans lost the first two sets of their semifinal match against Team USA in the 2012 Olympic semifinals. Then South Korea trailed by as many as six points in the third set. But the Asian team rallied. Before long the score was tied at 18. That is when Destinee Hooker took over.

The American outside hitter is one of the most athletic players in the world. She even won three college national championships in the high jump while at the University of Texas. Hooker ultimately decided to continue volleyball after college, though. And Team USA fans were glad she did.

Destinee Hooker rises high into the air to complete a hit during the gold-medal match at the 2012 Olympic Games.

With the score tied, the US setter prepared a back set. As she did, the 6-foot-4 Hooker began her approach. Hooker started a few feet behind the attack line and just out of bounds on the right side. Right on cue Hooker leapt into the air from five feet behind the net. At the peak of her jump, she struck the ball down with the palm of her right hand. The follow-through on her arm swing left some space between her hand and the net. Many players curl their body forward as they follow-through to try to get more oomph on the ball. But Hooker remains mostly upright. Her arm speed alone creates enough power.

Destinee Hooker gets tremendous power on her hits thanks to her long arms and great jumping ability.

Hooker's cross-court spike from the front right corner was too hard for the Korean defender to control. The pass attempt sailed out of bounds. The US won the next point to gain a two-point advantage. But South Korea soon pulled even again. Hooker responded with the same cross-court spike from the same spot aimed at the same defender. She achieved the same result.

Hooker had rotated to the back row when South Korea tied the score again at 21. But that did not matter. She refused to give the Koreans the lead. After a short rally, the Americans set a ball in the middle of their court. Hooker approached from her back-right position. She leapt from behind the attack line. Then she hit an off-speed spike toward the back left corner.

The change in pace caught the defenders off guard. Two Korean players watched the ball

HOOKER A JUMPER

Destinee Hooker's height (6 feet, 4 inches) makes her an ideal attacker. But her jumping ability sets her apart. She can jump 43 inches (109 cm) off the ground and reach up to 11 feet, 2 inches (3.35 m). That is almost four feet higher than a women's volleyball net at 7 feet, 4 1/8 inches (2.24 m). At the University of Texas, she won high jumping national titles in 2006, 2007, and 2009. And in 2008, she nearly qualified for the Olympic Games in high jumping. She placed sixth at the Olympic Trials but needed to be in the top three. With her height and jumping ability, she can often hit volleyballs completely over a block.

land safely in between them. They both threw their hands to their heads in disbelief. Three plays later, Hooker spiked again from the center of the back row. Her shot hit off a blocker and landed on the Korean side. That gave the Americans match point. They advanced to the gold-medal match on the next play.

Hooker finished the contest with 24 points. All but three of those points were from spikes. A spike that results in a point is called a kill. Hooker ranked second overall in scoring with 161 points in the 2012

Destinee Hooker, *right*, spikes the ball past South Korea's Kim Yeon-Koung during a match at the 2012 Olympic Games.

Olympic Games. She was named the tournament's Best Spiker. Hooker scored on 37.93 percent of her spike attempts. That proved to be crucial on Team USA's march to the silver medal.

Mastering the Spike

Spiking is the most exciting play in volleyball. It is the one skill that every young player wants to learn. But it is often the most difficult skill to master because it combines accuracy and strength. It is also a high-risk, high-reward play. It can immediately give your team a point if the spike lands in. But it can immediately give the other team a point if it lands out or in the net. Opposing teams can also take momentum if they block a spike.

For the best athletes, like Hooker, spiking involves jumping high above the net and smacking the ball toward the other team's court. The best players can jump very high. That allows them to drive the ball down with lots of power and a tight angle.

Spiking is a pretty advanced skill, though. Most kids learn how to execute a standing spike from 15 feet (4.58 m) behind the net. In doing this they try to hit the bottom third of the ball with the palm of their hand. Then they finish by snapping their wrists forward and pointing the fingers down. This creates topspin on the ball. Topspin makes the ball dip in flight so it is harder to dig.

With practice and growth, players can begin spiking closer to the net. Eventually players add an approach and jump. However, even the best players still sometimes use the standing spike in games. A player might not be able to make a good approach for a jump.

Players can also attack using off-speed hits. The roll shot is one example. It is carried out like a regular spike until the hitter eases up just before making contact. Instead she softly hits the ball with an open hand

Ma Yunwen, *right*, of China tips the ball over the hands of a Poland blocker during the 2008 Olympic Games in Beijing, China.

Quick Tip: One-on-One Drill

To practice hitting, grab another player and stand at the attack line on either side of the net. Together you two can play a one-on-one game. One player starts by tossing or serving the ball to the other. The partner then makes three contacts and sends it back over. Each player can pass and set to herself. Then work on the different types of hits: tips, roll shots, and spikes. Begin by performing each shot 10 times while standing, then do the same while jumping.

over or around the blockers. The key is to make it look exactly like a spike until the last moment.

Another off-speed hit is the open-handed tip. It is similar to the roll shot, but contact is made with the pads of the fingertips instead of the palm. The ball generally will not travel as far as a roll shot. An open-handed tip can take advantage of the empty space right behind the blockers. It is a touch shot that should just barely go over the blockers' hands and fall to the floor before any other defenders can reach it.

These off-speed shots are especially effective in beach volleyball. The defensive player in the back will often creep toward one side. If the attacker notices, she can poke the ball to the other side. Or if the back defender stays on one side, the hitter can attempt an open-handed tip to land immediately behind the blocker.

5

Blocking with
Kerri Walsh Jennings

I t was the first set of the 2012 Olympic beach volleyball gold-medal

match. Kerri Walsh Jennings stepped back to serve with a 12–11

lead. She put the ball in play. Then Walsh Jennings ran to the net and

watched the other team begin its play.

Fellow Americans Jennifer Kessy and April Ross received the serve. As

they went through the pass and set, Walsh Jennings positioned herself to

block the upcoming spike. Just before it came, Walsh Jennings planted her

feet. She raised both arms, bent them at the elbow, spread her fingers, and

brought her hands in front of her shoulders.

Kerri Walsh Jennings goes up for a block during the 2012 Olympic gold-medal match.

When the ball reached its highest point on the other side, Walsh Jennings squatted slightly. Then she jumped so her hands were in place right before the attacker struck the ball. In this instant, Walsh Jennings bent her upper body to the right while in the air. She wanted to take away the opponent's angle shot. It worked. Walsh Jennings reached over just far enough to get her fingertips on the ball. It landed on Kessy and Ross's side of the net. Walsh Jennings and partner Misty May-Treanor won the point. Then they went on to win the first set, 21–16.

In beach volleyball, teams play to the best of three sets. Walsh Jennings and May-Treanor pulled away to a 19–15 lead in the second set. They needed just two points to win the match when May-Treanor stepped back to serve. Walsh Jennings bent forward at the net and flashed a signal behind her back. She showed just her left index finger. This meant she would block toward the middle.

Walsh Jennings stayed bent over at the waist as the serve reached her opponents. She waited to see where the pass went. It traveled to her left, but the eventual attacker ran to Walsh Jennings's right. So she shuffled three times to her right as the set was sent into the air. On her last step, she planted her feet and jumped a split second after her opponent. Walsh Jennings bent to the left as she reached the peak of her jump. It was the correct guess. Ross spiked toward the middle of the court. But Walsh Jennings's hands beat the ball to the spot. It dropped quickly to the sand.

Walsh Jennings and May-Treanor went on to win the second set by the same score as the first, 21–16.

That victory marked the pair's third consecutive Olympic gold medal. Walsh Jennings's three blocks in the match gave her a total of 24 for the tournament. That was the most among all women. The International

Kerri Walsh Jennings leaps into the air after she and teammate Misty May-Treanor, *left*, won the 2012 Olympic gold medal.

After Kerri Walsh Jennings, Brazil's Juliana Silva is considered the next best beach volleyball blocker. Two of her biggest blocks came against Walsh Jennings and Misty May-Treanor in the 2011 Beach Volleyball World Championships final. The Americans led by four points in the third set. But Juliana and her partner, Larissa Franca, stormed back. It was tied at 14 when Juliana's right hand stopped a spike from Walsh Jennings. On the very next play, Juliana angled her block to the right again. This time she emphatically stopped a hit from May-Treanor. That gave the Brazilians their first world title.

Volleyball Federation later named her the Best Blocker in 2012. It was the sixth time in eight years that she received the honor. The beach volleyball legend was still as great as ever.

Blocking: The First Line of Defense

A volleyball team with strong offensive players is likely to score a lot of points. Of course, teams that score a lot of points win a lot of matches. But a squad can become even better if its defense scores, too. That means blocking.

Whether on a two-person beach volleyball team or a six-person indoor volleyball team, blocking is a key aspect of any game.

Blocking stops an opponent's shot from crossing the net. Sometimes the ball will fall to the court for a point. However, teams that get blocked can sometimes save the play and continue the rally. Blocks are often very sudden, though. That makes the opposing team more likely to make an error. It can also be frustrating to get blocked. So blocks can help build momentum for your team.

Blocking an opponent's shot involves timing, strength, and guesswork. A blocker first must watch the ball as the other team receives it. As the ball is set, blockers need to judge where it will come down. The quicker they

Indoor volleyball teams, such as China at the 2012 Olympic Games, often use several blockers to try to stop spikes.

can get to that spot, the better. This takes good side-to-side movement. To cover a short distance, blockers side-shuffle their feet while keeping their hands near their shoulders and their bodies facing the net. This side-to-side movement becomes more important when a team asks more than one player to block at a time. The blockers must move together.

A blocker must first get to the spot her opponent will hit from. Then the blocker plants her feet and squats. The lower a blocker squats, the higher she can jump. The goal is to jump straight up. The player must be careful to not let momentum carry her into the net or a teammate.

Kerri Walsh Jennings, *right*, executes a textbook block against an Australian team during the 2012 Olympic Games.

Quick Tip: Footwork Is Key

Blocking definitely takes skill. However, positioning is just as important. There are some easy ways to improve your side-to-side movement. One drill requires either a coach or a teammate to help. Have your partner stand on a chair on one side of the net, about 2 feet (.61 m) in from the sideline. Stand directly across the net. When your partner spikes, attempt to block it. Upon landing, sidestep to the near sideline, then sidestep back to the original position. Your partner then spikes again as you jump. Upon landing this time, crossover step toward the far sideline. Then crossover step back to the starting position.

As they jump, the blockers straighten and raise their arms and spread their fingers wide. They want to put as many body parts as possible in front of the shot. The blocker tries to reach the highest point of her jump when the opposing attacker hits the ball. The arms should slightly face downward so that a ball hitting them would be sent toward the ground. It is also important to keep the arms stiff because the force of a hard-driven ball can otherwise bend them backward. That could allow the ball to pass through.

Blocking might not be as essential as skills such as serving, passing, setting, and digging. However, as Walsh Jennings has proven, a team that can block is a team that is incredibly hard to beat.

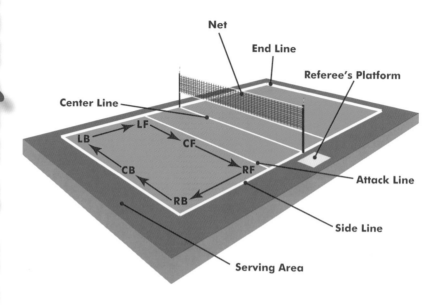

attack line

A line on the floor that runs parallel to the center and end lines on both sides of the court. It is 9 feet, 10 inches (3 meters) from the net and separates each side into a front zone and back zone.

back zone

The area of the court between the attack line and end line.

center line

The line that runs right under the net. It divides the court in half.

end line

The line at either end of the court that connects with the side lines. Serves must be taken from behind the end line.

front zone

The area of the court between the center line and attack line.

ace
> When a serve lands untouched in the opponent's court or the receiving team cannot make a play on its first touch.

approach
> The movements a player makes prior to jumping and hitting the ball.

assist
> The pass that comes immediately before a teammate successfully attacks.

attack
> When a player tries to score a point by hitting the ball over the net.

bump/dig
> Passing the ball by using the forearms with the hands together.

hold
> When the ball comes to a stop in a player's hands. This is also called a lift.

libero
> A ball control specialist who plays only in the back row, cannot hit the ball while it is higher than the net, cannot handset in front of the attack line, and wears a different colored jersey.

match
> An entire volleyball contest, which is made up of three beach sets or five indoor sets.

rally
> The series of actions two teams make to keep the ball in the air. When a rally ends, one team is awarded a point.

rotation
> The act of a team's six players moving from one position to the next in clockwise fashion. When a team earns a serve, each player moves one spot.

spike
> A hard-driven ball from a player's overhead swing that lands in the opponent's court. This is also called a kill.

Selected Bibliography

American Sport Education Program. *Coaching Youth Volleyball.* Champaign, IL: Human Kinetics, 2007.

USA Volleyball. *Volleyball Systems & Strategies.* Champaign, IL: Human Kinetics, 2009.

Zartman, Sharkie. *Youth Volleyball.* Cincinnati, OH: Writer's Digest Books, 2006.

Further Readings

Collin, Henry. *Volleyball: Playing with your Head at Any Height.* Terre Haute, IN: Wish Pub, 2005.

Crisfield, Deborah W., and John Monteleone. *Winning Volleyball for Girls.* New York: Chelsea House Publishers, 2010.

Poole, Jon R. *Volleyball: Mastering the Basics with the Personalized Sports Instruction System.* Boston: Allyn and Bacon, 2001.

Web Links

To learn more about volleyball, visit ABDO Publishing Company online at **www.abdopublishing.com**. Web sites about volleyball are featured on our Book Links page. These links are routinely monitored and updated to provide the most current information available.

Places to Visit

American Sports Centers
1500 S. Anaheim Blvd., Suite 110
Anaheim, CA 92805
(714) 917-3600
www.americansportscenters.com

American Sports Centers is home to the US men's and women's national volleyball teams, as well as numerous youth club volleyball teams. The facility includes 34 indoor volleyball courts and also features a sporting goods store with the top brands in volleyball.

Volleyball Hall of Fame
444 Dwight Street
Holyoke, MA 01040
(413) 536-0926
www.volleyhall.org

Learn about the greatest athletes to ever play the game of volleyball—in the town where the game started. The Volleyball Hall of Fame opened in 1987, and its first inductee was the late William G. Morgan, the inventor of volleyball. The Hall serves as a living memorial to the sport.

Index

ABOUT THE AUTHOR

Jon Ackerman has covered five Olympic Games for NBCOlympics.com. He focused on indoor and beach volleyball leading up to the Beijing 2008 and London 2012 Games. In Beijing and London, he was on-site at the beach volleyball venue. His volleyball writing has also appeared in *Volleyball Magazine* and on ESPN.com. He lives with his wife in Denver, Colorado.